SOLOS
for the
DOUBLE BASS PLAYER

With Piano Accompaniment

Selected and Edited by

OSCAR ZIMMERMAN

ED 2657

ISBN 978-1-5400-2818-1

G. SCHIRMER, *Inc.*
DISTRIBUTED BY
HAL•LEONARD®
7777 W. BLUEMOUND RD. P.O. BOX 13819 MILWAUKEE, WI 53213

www.musicsalesclassical.com
www.halleonard.com

CONTENTS

		Piano	Double Bass
BOURRÉE from Third Cello Suite	Johann Sebastian Bach	2	2
GRAVE	Evaristo Felice Dall'Abaco	5	3
CONCERTO (1st Movement from: *Violin* . . . . . . Concerto in A minor)	Antonio Vivaldi	7	4
PRELUDE AND ALLEGRO (from: *Sonata in* . . . . G Major)	Jean François d'Andrieu	13	7
SONATA IN C MINOR	George Frideric Handel	18	9
SONATINA	Ludwig van Beethoven	26	12
MINUET	Ludwig van Beethoven	28	13
ELEGY	Giovanni Bottesini	30	14
ANDANTE (from: *Concerto No. 2*)	Giovanni Bottesini	34	15
ARIA (from: *Rigoletto*)	Giuseppe Verdi	38	16
ADAGIO (from: *Concerto for Contrabass*)	Johann Geissel	42	17
VOCALISE	Serge Rachmaninoff	49	19
ROMANCE (from: *Lieutenant Kijé*)	Sergei Prokofiev	53	20
INTRODUCTION AND TARENTELLE	Carlo Franchi	57	21
SERENADE (from: *Sonata for Bass Viol and Piano*) .	Thomas Beveridge	70	25
CHACONNE	Armand Russell	75	27

Index by Composers

		Piano	Double Bass
EVARISTO FELICE DALL'ABACO	Grave	5	3
JEAN FRANÇOIS D'ANDRIEU	Prelude and Allegro (from: *Sonata in G Major*)	13	7
JOHANN SEBASTIAN BACH	Bourrée (from: *Third Cello Suite*)	2	2
LUDWIG VAN BEETHOVEN	Minuet	28	13
LUDWIG VAN BEETHOVEN	Sonatina	26	12
THOMAS BEVERIDGE	Serenade (from: *Sonata for Bass Viol and Piano*)	70	25
GIOVANNI BOTTESINI	Andante (from: *Concerto No. 2*)	34	15
GIOVANNI BOTTESINI	Elegy	30	14
CARLO FRANCHI	Introduction and Tarentelle	57	21
JOHANN GEISSEL	Adagio (from: *Concerto for Contrabass*)	42	17
GEORGE FRIDERIC HANDEL	Sonata in C minor	18	9
SERGEI PROKOFIEV	Romance (from: *Lieutenant Kijé*)	53	20
SERGE RACHMANINOFF	Vocalise	49	19
ARMAND RUSSELL	Chaconne	75	27
GIUSEPPE VERDI	Aria (from: *Rigoletto*)	38	16
ANTONIO VIVALDI	Allegro (1st Movement from: *Violin Concerto in A minor*)	7	4

1. Bourrée
from Third Cello Suite

Johann Sebastian Bach
(1685–1750)

2. Grave

Evaristo Felice Dall'Abaco
(1675–1742)

3. Allegro
from Violin Concerto in A minor

Antonio Vivaldi
(1678–1741)

4. Prelude and Allegro
from Sonata in G Major

Jean François d'Andrieu
(c.1682–1738)

Adagio

5. Sonata in C minor*

George Frideric Handel
(1685–1759)

* Originally written for oboe

Allegro

6. Sonatina

Ludwig van Beethoven
(1770–1827)

7. Minuet

Ludwig van Beethoven
(1770–1827)

8. Elegy

Giovanni Bottesini
(1821–1889)

9. Andante
from Concerto No. 2

Giovanni Bottesini
(1821–1889)

36

10. Aria
from *Rigoletto*

Giuseppe Verdi
(1813–1901)

SOLOS
for the
DOUBLE BASS
PLAYER

With Piano Accompaniment

Selected and Edited by

OSCAR ZIMMERMAN

ED 2657

ISBN 978-1-5400-2818-1

G. SCHIRMER, Inc.

DISTRIBUTED BY

7777 W. BLUEMOUND RD. P.O. BOX 13819 MILWAUKEE, WI 53213

www.musicsalesclassical.com
www.halleonard.com

CONTENTS

	Piano	Double Bass

BOURRÉE from Third Cello Suite . . . . Johann Sebastian Bach 2   2

GRAVE . . . . Evaristo Felice Dall'Abaco 5   3

CONCERTO (1st Movement from: *Violin* . . . . Antonio Vivaldi 7   4
     Concerto in A minor)

PRELUDE AND ALLEGRO (from: *Sonata in* . . . . Jean François d'Andrieu 13   7
     G Major)

SONATA IN C MINOR . . . . George Frideric Handel 18   9

SONATINA . . . . Ludwig van Beethoven 26   12

MINUET . . . . Ludwig van Beethoven 28   13

ELEGY . . . . Giovanni Bottesini 30   14

ANDANTE (from: *Concerto No. 2*) . . . . Giovanni Bottesini 34   15

ARIA (from: *Rigoletto*) . . . . Giuseppe Verdi 38   16

ADAGIO (from: *Concerto for Contrabass*) . . . . . Johann Geissel 42   17

VOCALISE . . . . Serge Rachmaninoff 49   19

ROMANCE (from: *Lieutenant Kijé*) . . . . Sergei Prokofiev 53   20

INTRODUCTION AND TARENTELLE . . . . Carlo Franchi 57   21

SERENADE (from: *Sonata for Bass Viol and Piano*) . Thomas Beveridge 70   25

CHACONNE . . . . Armand Russell 75   27

Index by Composers

		Piano	Double Bass
EVARISTO FELICE DALL'ABACO	Grave	5	3
JEAN FRANÇOIS D'ANDRIEU	Prelude and Allegro (from: *Sonata in G Major*)	13	7
JOHANN SEBASTIAN BACH	Bourrée (from: *Third Cello Suite*)	2	2
LUDWIG VAN BEETHOVEN	Minuet	28	13
LUDWIG VAN BEETHOVEN	Sonatina	26	12
THOMAS BEVERIDGE	Serenade (from: *Sonata for Bass Viol and Piano*)	70	25
GIOVANNI BOTTESINI	Andante (from: *Concerto No. 2*)	34	15
GIOVANNI BOTTESINI	Elegy	30	14
CARLO FRANCHI	Introduction and Tarentelle	57	21
JOHANN GEISSEL	Adagio (from: *Concerto for Contrabass*)	42	17
GEORGE FRIDERIC HANDEL	Sonata in C minor	18	9
SERGEI PROKOFIEV	Romance (from: *Lieutenant Kijé*)	53	20
SERGE RACHMANINOFF	Vocalise	49	19
ARMAND RUSSELL	Chaconne	75	27
GIUSEPPE VERDI	Aria (from: *Rigoletto*)	38	16
ANTONIO VIVALDI	Allegro (1st Movement from: *Violin Concerto in A minor*)	7	4

2

1. Bourrée
from Third Cello Suite

Johann Sebastian Bach
(1685–1750)

Allegro moderato

2. Grave

Evaristo Felice Dall'Abaco
(1675–1742)

3. Allegro
from Violin Concerto in A minor

Antonio Vivaldi
(1678–1741)

4. Prelude and Allegro
from Sonata in G Major

Jean François d'Andrieu
(c.1682–1738)

8

5. Sonata in C minor★

George Frideric Handel
(1685–1759)

★ Originally written for Oboe

6. Sonatina

Ludwig van Beethoven
(1770–1827)

7. Minuet

Ludwig van Beethoven
(1770–1827)

Minuetto D. C.
senza repetizione

8. Elegy

Giovanni Bottesini
(1821–1889)

14

9. Andante
from Concerto No. 2

Giovanni Bottesini
(1821–1889)

10. Aria
from *Rigoletto*

Giuseppe Verdi
(1813–1901)

11. Adagio
from Concerto for Contrabass, Op. 32

Johann Geissel
(1796–1864)

Cadenza ad lib.

rit.

Un poco animato

poco a poco rit.

a tempo

rit. poco a poco

Tempo I

rit.

12. Vocalise
Op. 34, No. 14

Serge Rachmaninoff
(1873–1943)

13. Romance
from *Lieutenant Kijé*

Sergei Prokofiev
(1891–1953)

14. Introduction and Tarentelle

Carlo Franchi
(1743?–1779?)

15. Serenade
from Sonata for Bass Viol and Piano

Thomas Beveridge
(b. 1938)

* slide without striking second time.

16. Chaconne

Armand Russell
(b. 1932)

11. Adagio
from Concerto for Contrabass, Op. 32

Johann Geissel
(1796–1864)

Cadenza ad lib.

Un poco animato

12. Vocalise
Op. 34, No. 14

Serge Rachmaninoff
(1873–1943)

52

13. Romance

from *Lieutenant Kijé*

Sergei Prokofiev
(1891–1953)

55

56

14. Introduction and Tarentelle

Carlo Franchi
(1743?–1779?)

61

65

15. Serenade
from Sonata for Bass Viol and Piano

Thomas Beveridge
(b. 1938)

16. Chaconne

Armand Russell
(b. 1932)